A New Beginning

A New Beginning

An ESL Reader

Mary Mitchell Church

Keesia Harrison Hyzer

Ann Marie Niedermeier

Madison Metropolitan Schools
Madison, Wisconsin

Illustrated by
Jana Fothergill

PRENTICE HALL REGENTS
Englewood Cliffs, New Jersey 07632

Library of Congress Cataloging-in-Publication Data

Church, Mary Mitchell.
  A new beginning.

  1. English language—Textbooks for foreign speakers.
  2. Readers—1950–   . I. Hyzer, Keesia Harrison.
  II. Niedermeier, Ann Marie. III. Title.
  PE1128.C583 1988   428.6'4   88–5933
  ISBN 0–13–611849–6

Cover designer: Diane Saxe
Manufacturing buyer: Peter Havens

 © 1988 by Prentice-Hall, Inc.
A Division of Simon & Schuster
Englewood Cliffs, New Jersey 07632

Printed in the United States of America
10 9 8 7 6 5 4 3 2 1

ISBN 0-13-611849-6

Prentice-Hall International (UK) Limited, *London*
Prentice-Hall of Australia Pty. Limited, *Sydney*
Prentice-Hall Canada Inc., *Toronto*
Prentice-Hall Hispanoamericana, S.A., *Mexico*
Prentice-Hall of India Private Limited, *New Delhi*
Prentice-Hall of Japan, Inc., *Tokyo*
Simon & Schuster Asia Pte. Ltd., *Singapore*
Editora Prentice-Hall do Brasil, Ltda., *Rio de Janeiro*

We wish to dedicate this reading text to our students, whose hard work, determination, and general good humor motivated us to write a beginning-level book for them, and to our families, who have supported us throughout.

Contents

Introduction

A New Beginning: An ESL Reader is a comprehensive reading book for secondary and adult students of English as a Second Language at the advanced beginning or low intermediate level. It focuses on reading but includes listening, speaking, and writing exercises. The reading passages in each chapter feature a Central American family recently arrived in the United States. The chapters are based on the experiences of immigrant families in order to promote student interest and aid in comprehension of the readings.

In this text, reading is an active, problem-solving process that includes pre-reading, reading, and follow-up. During pre-reading, students organize for the reading experience by brainstorming about the topic and learning essential vocabulary. The readings are designed to help students enjoy reading as well as expand their communicative vocabulary and cultural knowledge. The post-reading activities, including comprehension, listening, speaking, and writing, reflect the philosophy that these skills are interrelated and enhance comprehension. Grammar and vocabulary are controlled, but students are exposed to real language at different levels.

Many exercises are included, so teachers can select from them according to the level of their classes. All teachers will not use all exercises. However, we encourage teachers to try exercises that at first seem difficult; field testing has shown that they are successful with even very low-level classes. Students need not have mastered every grammar point, not even past tense, before reading many of the selections.

Teaching Suggestions

During **pre-reading**, students get ready to read by exploring the general topic of the chapter. The questions in this section stimulate classroom discussion so that students can relate the topic of the reading passage to their own experience. At this time, students should be encouraged to make predictions about the reading passage. The **vocabulary** that students need for the reading passage is included in the pre-reading section. Targeted vocabulary items are italicized when they appear in exercises. Many of these words are illustrated in the artwork that accompanies the reading. There is also a vocabulary section after the reading passage. Some teachers, however, may want to do all the vocabulary work before starting the reading passage. Teachers should help students guess at the meaning of new words so the students can gain independence in their reading skills. Teachers are encouraged to include simple word games like password, word bingo, concentration, vocabulary tic-tac-toe, and jeopardy even when they are not mentioned in the text. Students of all ages enjoy these games, which require a minimum of teacher preparation time. (See Appendix 2, Word Games.)

The **reading passage** should first be presented in its entirety. Students at this level will benefit from hearing the teacher read the passage to them as they follow along, reading silently. The **comprehension** section immediately following the reading passage includes some questions that require factual answers and others that are more challenging. Both types of questions are suitable for homework. Some teachers will want to do the comprehension work orally in class and assign the same question for homework.

The **listening, conversation,** and **writing** sections recycle the vocabulary of the reading passages. For some listening exercises, the students will be directed to close their books. They listen as the teacher reads a passage, then answer questions. The conversation section is interactive. Teachers are encouraged to have students work in pairs or small groups whenever possible. Many of the exercises lend themselves to role-play, and students may enjoy using some simple props to enhance role-play situations. Teachers are encouraged to adapt favorite games to the topics and exercises in the text.

In these sections, students discuss the chapter topic in greater depth and are given a chance to compare cultures. These discussions are often the basis for the writing exercises that follow. Many of the writing exercises, especially the second exercise in the writing section, are also suitable for homework.

In the reading practice section, there are additional reading passages in varied forms to be read in a less intensive way. Readings from real life, such as product labels or rules, give students practice in becoming independent readers.

1

Moving In

Pre-reading

A. What do you think?

1. Why are there so many boxes in this apartment?
2. Who are these people? Can you guess where they are from? Can you guess their ages? Can you guess how they feel?

3. Why do people move to a new country?
4. What is good about moving to a new country?
5. What is hard about moving to a new country?

B. What does it mean? Can you guess what the italicized words mean?

1. This family came to the United States the day before yesterday. They *arrived* two days *ago*.
2. They will not go back to their country. They *plan* to stay in the United States *forever*.
3. Mom is a little afraid about the United States. She feels *nervous* about the United States.
4. Carlos is tired, so he is *taking a break* from work. He is sitting down in a chair.
5. They found an apartment fast, so they feel *lucky*.
6. Mom is a little *homesick*. She *misses* her country a lot.
7. Carlos will study at a *technical college*.

Reading

MOVING IN

Mrs. Ana Gonzalez and her two children, Carlos and Rosa, arrived in Madison, Wisconsin, two days ago. They are from Central America but plan to stay in the United States forever. They all know a little English, but they want to learn more.

Carlos is twenty-one and his sister, Rosa, is seventeen. Their grandfather will come to Madison to live with them soon. Carlos and Rosa want to learn a lot of English before he comes so they can help him. Their grandfather doesn't speak any English.

Mrs. Gonzalez feels nervous about the United States. She is alone with her children because her husband died a year ago.

Carlos is tired, so he is taking a break from moving. He is writing a letter to his English class back home. Read the letter and think about Ana, Carlos, and Rosa.

August 20

Dear Mrs. Gomez and English students,

We are finally here in Madison! The city is small but beautiful. We found an apartment fast, so we feel lucky.

Mom thinks English is hard. Rosa and I understand a lot, but we make a lot of mistakes and we get tired.

School opens in two weeks. Rosa will go to high school and I will go to technical college. Mom plans to find a job. She will take some English classes at night, too.

Rosa loves the United States! Mom is a little homesick. She misses our country a lot. She will be happy when Grandpa comes. Everything is different, but I think I will like the United States.

Please write soon. Remember to write in English!

Your friend,
Carlos

Comprehension

C. Answer these questions. Some questions have more than one answer.

1. Where is this family from?
2. Where will they live in the United States?
3. How long will they stay in the United States?
4. How old are Carlos and Rosa? Where will they go to school?
5. Who will come to live with them soon?
6. Did Ana's husband come with them? Why or why not?
7. Does Rosa like the United States?
8. What does Carlos think about the United States?
9. When will Ana feel happy?

D. Read the story again. Then write three things about each person.

Ana	*Rosa*	*Carlos*
a mother		
nervous		

Vocabulary

E. Read and discuss these words. Then write the correct word in each blank.

plan   lucky
forever   technical college
nervous

1. Some people feel ___*lucky*___ when they find some money on the street.
2. They want to stay in the United States _____.
3. After high school, some students go to a _____. People of all ages study there.
4. Ana feels _____ about the United States.
5. Rosa, Carlos, and Ana _____ to learn more English.

F. Find a sentence on the right that means the same as a sentence on the left. Write the correct letter in the blank.

_f_ 1. Ana feels *nervous*.
___ 2. They *arrived* one year *ago*.
___ 3. Ana is *homesick*.
___ 4. Carlos is *taking a break*.
___ 5. He was a farmer *back home*.
___ 6. They found an apartment *fast*.

a. Ana *misses* her country.
b. They came at this time last year.
c. They found an apartment quickly.
d. Carlos is not working now. He is resting.
e. He was a farmer in his country.
f. Ana doesn't feel comfortable.

Listening

G. Books closed. Number your paper from 1 to 6. Your teacher will read six sentences about the Gonzalez family. Write *T* for a true sentence or *F* for a false sentence. Open your book and look at "Moving In" to check your answers.

1. The Gonzalez family is from New York.
2. Ana, Carlos, and Rosa all know a little English.
3. Carlos is writing a letter in English.
4. They are moving into a big house.
5. They plan to stay in the United States forever.
6. Ana has a job.

Conversation

H. Practice asking and answering questions about where places are.

Example: Where is _the bus stop?_____?
_It's just around the corner._____

1. Pardon me. Where is _____?

_____

2. Excuse me, please. Where is _____?

_____

3. How can I find _____?

_____

I. Below is a drawing of an apartment. Talk about each room and what people do in that room.

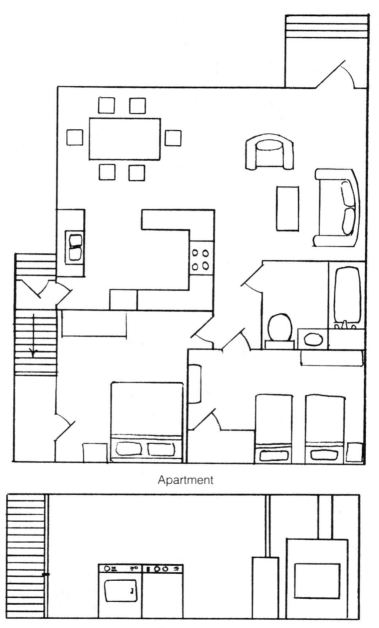

Apartment

Basement

Now find the room on the right that goes with the activity on the left. Write the correct letter in the blank.

_a_ 1. You pay rent each   a. an apartment
     month to live here.   b. a bathroom
___ 2. You cook and   c. a kitchen
     sometimes eat here.   d. a basement
___ 3. You sleep here.   e. a bedroom
___ 4. You watch TV, read, or   f. a dining area
     talk here.   g. a living room
___ 5. You take a shower here.
___ 6. You eat in this place,
     but you don't wash
     dishes here.
___ 7. This is under a house,
     and you wash clothes
     here.

Writing

J. Look at the drawing in (I) again. Think about where you live, too. What do you find in each room? Read the words below and write them in the blank under the correct room. Some words can go under two rooms. Add words of your own, too.

bed   table and chairs   couch
sink   shower   bathtub
stove   dresser   refrigerator
TV

Kitchen	Bedroom	Bathroom	Living Room	Dining Area
_____	_____	_____	_____	_____
_____	_____	_____	_____	_____
_____	_____	_____	_____	_____
_____	_____	_____	_____	_____

K. Read Carlos's letter again. Then write to one of your friends in English. Tell about your life in the United States by completing the sentences below.

_____, 19____

Dear _____,

    I am here in _____. It is _____.

    I think English is _____. I understand

_____ and I make some mistakes.

    I go to _____ school. My English class is

_____.

    My life is _____ here. I think the United States is

_____.

Your friend,

_____

Reading Practice

L. These are rules about the Gonzalez's new apartment. Read and discuss them with your classmates.

APARTMENT RULES

1. No pets.
2. Pay rent on first day of month.
3. Pay rent by check or money order. No cash.
4. Put trash in trash cans only.
5. No vegetable gardens in front yard.
6. Only two people for each bedroom.
7. Visitors cannot stay over two weeks.
8. Keep basement clean.
9. Watch children carefully.

Now answer these questions about the rules.

1. How many people can sleep in each bedroom?
2. When do you pay your rent?
3. How can you pay your rent?
4. Can you have a dog in your apartment?
5. Where should you put trash?
6. Can you have a garden in your front yard?
7. How long can a visitor stay?
8. Who cleans the basement?
9. Do you have rules like this where you live? Find out and write two of them down. Bring them to class and talk about them.

2

A New Beginning

Pre-Reading

A. What do you think?

1. Where are these people?
2. How old are they? Are they *adults*?
3. How do they feel? How do you know?

4. Who is coming into the room?
5. What does the title "A New Beginning" mean?
6. Think about your first day in a new school. How did you feel?

B. What does it mean? Can you guess what the italicized words mean?

I went to a party at a new friend's apartment. The apartment was in a big old (1) *building*, and it was hard to find. I walked into the party and saw only (2) *strangers*. I didn't know anyone, and I felt nervous and (3) *alone*. Then I (4) *introduced* myself to some people, and then to some more people. There were people from (5) *all over the world*, and soon we all felt (6) *comfortable*. What a (7) *surprise*—I had a lot of fun.

Reading

Ana is taking ESL night classes for adults at a technical college. Her homework is to write about her first ESL class. Read her story and think about your first ESL class.

A NEW BEGINNING

Ana Gonzalez

In September I started school again, but this time in the United States. The school building, classrooms, students—everything—was new and different. In the halls, I saw all kinds of strangers. I didn't know anyone. I felt very alone.

That first night, I looked for the ESL classroom. I walked into the room and saw students from all over the world. What a surprise! I wanted to know where they all came from.

I sat down and waited for the teacher. Everyone was quiet. We all felt nervous. After a while, the teacher came, and we all introduced ourselves. Soon, everyone smiled and looked comfortable. The teacher gave us some books, and we studied the first three pages.

At the end of class, people talked to each other. We all

had some new books and some new friends. It was a new beginning for all of us.

Comprehension

C. Write *T* before the true sentences and *F* before the false sentences.

___ 1. Ana went to day classes.
___ 2. School in Ana's country is the same as school in the United States.
___ 3. The students were from all over the world.
___ 4. At first, the students all felt comfortable.
___ 5. At the end of class, they all had some new friends.

D. Answer the questions about the story.

1. What kind of school is Ana going to?
2. What kind of classes is she taking? Can she take other classes at that school?
3. Tell three feelings she had the first night of classes. Example: Ana felt surprised.
4. Tell two things the students did in class.
5. When did the students begin to feel comfortable? Why?

Vocabulary

E. Find a sentence on the right that means the same as the sentence on the left. Write the correct letter in the blank.

___ 1. He is a *stranger*.
___ 2. I feel *comfortable*.
___ 3. We *introduced* ourselves.
___ 4. I am *alone*.
___ 5. Ana is an *adult*.

a. He told me his name, and I told him my name.
b. I don't know him.
c. I have no friends.
d. I feel OK. I don't feel nervous or afraid.
e. Ana is over 18.

F. Read the vocabulary words again and make a sentence with each one. Your teacher will write your sentences on the board. Practice reading them.

adults   comfortable
building   all over the world
alone   to introduce
strangers   surprise

Conversation

G. Talk about your first day of school in this country. With a partner, practice asking and answering the questions below. Then tell the class about your partner.

1. When did you come to the United States?

_____

2. When was your first day of school in this country?

_____

3. How is this school different from school in your country?

_____

4. Did you like your new school at first? Why or why not?

_____

H. Problem Solving. These are some problems new students sometimes have. What can you do about the problems? Talk about them and write your ideas on the blackboard.

Problem	*What to Do*
Example: Lee can't understand one of his teachers.	*Lee goes to talk to his teacher*
	_____

1. Chen can't find the classroom.

1. _____
   _____

2. Anita never practices English outside of class.

2. _____
   _____

3. Huan is so homesick he can't think about English.

3. _____
   _____

4. Danielle comes to only half the classes.

4. _____
   _____

5. Mai is very shy. She's afraid to speak English to anyone.

5. _____
   _____

Writing

I. In groups of two, write a dialogue about one of the problems in (H), above. Your dialogue should have about six lines. Later, you can act out the dialogue for your class.

> **Example:** Problem: Mai is very shy. She's afraid to speak English to anyone.

Dialogue:

Teacher: Mai, please speak more in class. You can feel comfortable here.

Mai: But I always make mistakes.

Teacher: That's OK. Everyone makes mistakes. I make mistakes every day, and English is my first language.

Mai: But I don't know what to say.

Teacher: Just try! Everyone feels nervous and shy at first, but practice helps those feelings go away.

Mai: OK, I'll try.

J. Read "A New Beginning" again. Then fill in the blanks below with words that make this story true for you.

A NEW BEGINNING

_____
(your name)

Yesterday was my first day of classes. The school building is very _____. I didn't know anyone, and I got lost. I felt very _____. Then I found the ESL class. The other ESL students were _____. The teacher was very _____ and I liked him very much.

Now when I go to class I feel _____. I want to study hard and learn _____.

Listening

K. Practice reading your story (from J) aloud. Then read your story to the class. Your teacher will ask the class questions about the story you read.

L. Write four sentences about yourself. The teacher will read them to the class. Then the class will guess who you are.

Example: I am fifty-four years old.
I am a man.
I have short, black hair.
I am wearing black shoes.

1. _____

2. _____

3. _____

4. _____

Reading Practice

M. Find the answer on the right that matches the question on the left. Write the correct letter in the blank.

___ 1. What's your name?	a. It's 12 o'clock noon.
___ 2. What is your birthdate?	b. It's down the hall, on the left.
___ 3. Where's the ESL classroom?	c. I'm from Mexico.
___ 4. Where are you from?	d. I live at 1312 Main Street.
___ 5. How long have you been here?	e. My name's Bertha.
	f. It's area code 608-222-1423.
___ 6. Are you married?	g. I've been here five months.
___ 7. What is your first language?	h. I was born March 10, 1940.
___ 8. What's your address?	i. I speak Spanish.
___ 9. What's your phone number?	j. No, I'm single.
___ 10. What time is it, please?	

3

Ready to Work

Pre-reading

A. What do you think?

1. How can you find a job? Make a list of ways to find a job.
2. Who has a job in your class? Ask those people these questions:
   a. Did you need work experience (practice at a job)?
   b. How many years of school did you need?
   c. How did you find your job?
   d. Did you have a *job interview*?
3. What kind of job do you want? How can you get ready for that job?

B. What does it mean? Find a sentence on the right that has the same meaning as a sentence on the left. Write the correct letter in the blank.

____ 1. Carlos *would rather* have a job than go to school.

____ 2. You *have to* go now.

____ 3. *Are you sure?*

____ 4. Are we *ready* to go?

____ 5. Ana needs to *earn* some money.

____ 6. I want to *quit* smoking.

____ 7. You *forgot* my name.

a. You need to go now.

b. I want to stop smoking.

c. Are you certain?

d. Carlos wants to get a job instead of going to school.

e. Ana needs to work to get money.

f. Can we go now?

g. You didn't remember my name.

Reading

READY TO WORK

Mom: Oh, no! I can't find my green dress! Rosa, do you know where it is?

Rosa: It's in my closet, Mom. Why are you so nervous?

Mom: Don't you remember? Today is my job interview at the Hotel Madison!

Rosa: Oh, that's right.

Mom: I really want a job. I want to take care of the family by myself.

Carlos: Are you sure? Maybe I should quit school and get a job.

Mom: No, Carlos. I want you to stay in school. For now, I'll work and earn money for the family. But you and Rosa have to help more with the housework.

Carlos: I would rather get a job!

Mom: Well, I'm ready. How do I look?

Rosa: You look just great, Mom. But you forgot one thing.

Mom: What?

Rosa: Your shoes!

Comprehension

C. Answer these questions about "Ready to Work."

1. How does Mom feel? Why?
2. Why does Mom want to get a job?
3. For now, Carlos will not get a job. Why not?
4. Does Carlos like housework? How do you know?
5. What did Mom forget? Why?

D. Can you answer these questions? Some questions will have more than one answer.

1. Why is Mom's dress in Rosa's closet?
2. Are there other ways for Mom to take care of the family?
3. Why do Carlos and Rosa have to help more with the housework?

Vocabulary

E. Find these expressions in the dialogue. Then write sentences of your own using the expressions. Write your sentences on the blackboard, and then practice reading them.

1. take care of
2. stay in school
3. by myself
4. would rather
5. get a job

F. Who am I? Find a job on the right that means the same as the definition on the left. Write the correct letter in the blank.

_____ 1. I work in a garage. I fix cars.

_____ 2. I work in a hospital or clinic. I help patients and doctors.

_____ 3. I take letters and magazines to houses, apartments, and businesses.

_____ 4. I clean the offices in a large building.

_____ 5. I work in a school. I help people learn.

_____ 6. I take children to school every day in a school bus.

_____ 7. I take food to people in a restaurant.

a. teacher
b. nurse
c. auto mechanic
d. bus driver
e. janitor
f. mail carrier
g. waiter

Conversation

G. Make a list of jobs. List all kinds of jobs. Then talk about the experience and education you need for each one. On the blackboard make a chart like this:

Job	Experience you need	Education you need
auto mechanic	some experience working on cars	high school education, auto mechanics class

Listening

H. Books closed. Listen to this conversation. Then you will hear three questions about the conversation. Write your answers. Open your book to check them.

> *Dan:* Hi, Carlos. Did your mom get the job?
>
> *Carlos:* Yes, she did. She's really happy about it. Now she can earn money for the family.
>
> *Dan:* And you can stay in school!
>
> *Carlos:* Yes, Mom is working because she wants me to go to school. Now I don't have to quit, but I do have to study hard.

1. Who got the job?
2. How does she feel?
3. Who will quit school?

Writing

I. This is some information about Mom. Discuss this information with your class. Then help Mom fill out the job application below.

Ana Gonzalez   Telephone: 608-231-0492
612 Lakeside Apts.   Height: 5'3"
Madison, WI 53705   Weight: 140
Date of Birth: September 12, 1940
Schooling: through grade 5
Work experience: mother and housewife
Reference: Kathy Dunn, 406 Kendall Ave., Madison, WI
                53705, 238-7741 (ESL teacher)

Job Application—Hotel Madison

General information

_____

last name   first name   middle initial

_____

street address   city   state   zip code

_____

phone number   date of birth   sex

_____

height   weight

What job are you applying for?_____

Education

Circle your last year of education

   1 2 3 4 5   6 7 8   9 10 11 12   1 2 3 4 5
    elementary   middle school   high school   college

Work experience

Name of Company   Location   Position   Dates

1. _____

2. _____

References

     Name   Address   Phone

1. _____

2. _____

3. _____

Signature _____ Date _____

J. Read this dialogue. This is part of Ana's job interview at the Hotel Madison. First discuss these words:

application (to apply)　　interviewer　　maid

Interviewer:　Good morning, Mrs. Gonzalez. I'm Lidia Lopez. Please sit down. What can I do for you?

Ana:　I want to apply for a job.

Interviewer:　Which one?

Ana:　Maid.

Interviewer:　OK. Let me ask you a few questions. Have you had a job before?

Ana:　No, I haven't. Is that necessary?

Interviewer:　No, not at all. Now, tell me, what hours can you work?

Ana:　I can work any time. I need to have a job.

As a class, think of one more question for the interviewer to ask Ana. Write the question and Ana's answer below.

Interviewer:　_____ ?

Ana:　_____

Now practice reading the dialogue with a classmate.

Reading Practice

K. Below are some job advertisements from a newspaper. Read each advertisement with your classmates and then answer these questions about each one:

1. Do you need experience for this job?
2. Is the job full-time or part-time?
3. Can *you* do this job? Why or why not?

Bike mechanic Full- or part-time, experience necessary. Apply to: Madison Cycle 508 Tenth St. 53711	**Nurses' Aides** Part-time, will train. $4.30/hour starting. Apply to: Lakewood Nursing Home 3801 Lake Ave., 53705
Office cleaning Full-time days. Call Rita, 233-5346	**Bank teller** Full-time, Experience necessary. Apply to: Hilldale Bank Box 412, 53711
Restaurant Help Openings for early mornings. The Sandwich Shop, 3342 W. School Avenue.	**Cooks and Dishwashers** Full- and part-time. 835-3086.

4

Keep Your Eyes on the Road

Pre-reading

A. What does it mean? Find a word below that matches something in the picture above.

traffic light
corner

B. What do you think? Answer these questions about the picture.

1. Why does the car have a sign on it?
2. Who has a driver's license? Did she have to take driving lessons?

Reading

KEEP YOUR EYES ON THE ROAD

Mr. Martin: Hi, Carlos! Are you ready for your driving lesson?

Carlos: I sure am! Where will we go today?

Mr. Martin: First, let's drive up to the corner and turn right.

Carlos: How am I doing?

Mr. Martin: Good, but slow down a little.

Carlos: Look! There's my sister, Rosa, at the bus stop!

Mr. Martin: Carlos! Don't look at your sister! Watch the road!

Carlos: Sorry, Mr. Martin.

Mr. Martin: That's better. Remember, always keep your eyes on the road. Look! The traffic light is yellow.

Carlos: OK. I'll go faster.

Mr. Martin: No! Slow down, Carlos! The light will turn red in a second.

(The light turns red but Carlos doesn't stop.)

Carlos: Whoops! Too late! I'm not doing very well today, am I? Are you all right, Mr. Martin?

Mr. Martin: Yes, I'm fine. I'm just glad to be alive!

Comprehension

C. Write *T* before the true sentences and *F* before the false sentences.

_____ 1. Carlos is a very good driver.
_____ 2. Carlos always watches the road.
_____ 3. A yellow light means that the light will turn red soon.
_____ 4. Carlos drives too slowly.
_____ 5. Carlos doesn't stop at the red traffic light.

D. Books closed. Take out a piece of paper. Your teacher will read the lines below, which are from the dialogue. If Carlos said the line, write *Carlos*. If Mr. Martin said the line, write *Mr. Martin*. Then open your book and check your answers by looking at the dialogue.

1. "Yes, I'm fine. I'm just glad to be alive!"
2. "How am I doing?"
3. "OK. I'll go faster."
4. "That's better. Remember, always keep your eyes on the road."
5. "Good, but slow down a little."

Vocabulary

E. Find a word or phrase on the right that means the same as the word or phrase on the left. Write the correct letter in the blank.

_____ 1. traffic light
_____ 2. slow down
_____ 3. instructor
_____ 4. road
_____ 5. keep your eyes on the road
_____ 6. alive

a. watch the road
b. teacher
c. don't go so fast
d. stoplight
e. street
f. not dead, living

F. Write a dialogue using the words and phrases below. Your teacher will write your sentences on the blackboard. Then practice reading them.

1. all right
2. sorry
3. in a second
4. remember
5. close to

Listening

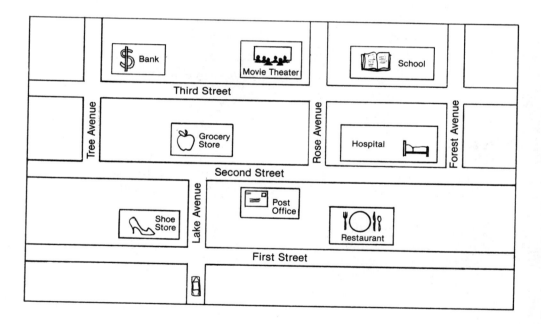

G. Find the car on Lake Avenue. You are the driver of the car and your teacher will tell you where to go. Don't look at the directions; just listen carefully!

1. Go straight on Lake Avenue.
2. Go left on Second Street.
3. Turn right on Tree Avenue.
4. Turn right again on Third Street.
5. Turn left on Rose Avenue and stop.
   Where are you?

Now, working in pairs, practice giving each other directions to some of the places on the map.

H. Your teacher will read the first five lines of "Keep Your Eyes on the Road." Listen carefully and write on the lines below.

Mr. Martin: _____

Carlos: _____

Mr. Martin: _____

_____

Carlos: _____

Mr. Martin: _____

Now read the sentences back to your teacher, who will write them on the blackboard. Then practice reading the lines.

Conversation

I. Work in pairs or small groups and answer the following questions about the signs on page 31.

1. What does this sign mean? Write the meaning under each picture.
2. Where do you usually see this sign?

J. Find someone in your class who has a driver's license (maybe your teacher). Take turns asking the following questions.

1. How long have you been driving?
2. How did you learn to drive?
3. When you got your driver's license, which test was more difficult—the driving test or the written test?
4. Did you pass your driving test the first time?
5. Do you have car insurance? Why or why not?

K. This is Mr. Martin's driver's license. Discuss the information on his license.

DATE OF BIRTH 11/6/48		LICENSE NUMBER L–421–441–6291		EXPIRATION DATE 11/6/89
SEX M	EYES BR	HAIR BR	WEIGHT 185	HEIGHT 5'11"
Gerald F. Martin 842 Mineral Point Rd. Madison, WI 53705 *Gerald F. Martin* SIGNATURE				

Now, working in pairs, answer these questions about Mr. Martin's license. One person can ask the question and the other person can answer. For homework, write the answers.

1. How old is Mr. Martin?
2. What is his address?
3. What color are Mr. Martin's eyes and hair?

1. _____ 2. _____ 3. _____ 4. _____

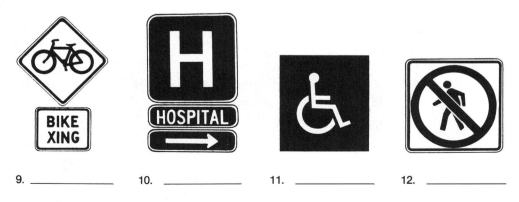

5. _____ 6. _____ 7. _____ 8. _____

9. _____ 10. _____ 11. _____ 12. _____

31

4. When does Mr. Martin need to get a new license?
5. How much does Mr. Martin weigh?

Writing

L. This is *your* driver's license. Fill in the information about your-self.

OPERATOR'S LICENSE		REGULAR
DATE OF BIRTH	LICENSE NUMBER L-293-339-4938	EXPIRATION DATE 6/10/95

SEX	EYES	HAIR	WEIGHT	HEIGHT
——	——	——	——	——

NAME AND ADDRESSS

SIGNATURE

Reading Practice

M. This is a poem about traffic lights. Read it with your classmates. Practice it at home and then teach it to a child you know.

Red on top and green below.
Red says "STOP" and green says "GO."
Yellow says "WAIT" even if you're late!

N. Carlos is writing a letter for homework for his English class. The letter is to his cousin Pedro, who lives in Chicago.

Dear Pedro,

    Guess what! I got my driver's license! I passed my test yesterday. First I had to take a written test. I didn't pass it the first time. I studied a lot, but the test was difficult. Then I took the test again, and the second time I passed! The driving test was easy. My driving lessons with Mr. Martin really helped.

    Now all we need is a car! Mom has a job now, so maybe we can save money for a used car.

    How is your family? Write soon! When we get a car, I'll drive to Chicago to see you!

Your friend,
Carlos

Find these phrases in the letter, and with your classmates try to guess what they mean.

to pass a test	a used car	a written test
to save money	Guess what!	

Answer these questions about the letter:

1. What tests did Carlos have to take?
2. Which test was easy? Which was difficult?
3. What does Carlos need now?
4. Will Carlos buy a new car? Why?
5. How do you think Carlos feels?

5

Running Is for Rabbits

Pre-reading

A. What do you think?

1. Why do people exercise?
2. Do many people in your country like to exercise?
   Do older people exercise or only young people?

3. Do you do any kinds of exercise? What kinds?
4. Why do people like to jog? Do people jog in your country?
5. On the blackboard, make a list of different kinds of exercise. Talk about why they are good for your health.

B. What does it mean? Can you guess what the italicized words mean?

1. The men are *jogging*.
2. Carlos is wearing *running shoes*.
3. Carlos is wearing a *sweatshirt*.

Reading

RUNNING IS FOR RABBITS

Carlos has an American teacher who likes to jog. His name is Rick. The first month of school, Carlos saw Rick jogging down the street in his sweatshirt, sweatpants, and running shoes each day after class. Carlos thought, "Why does he like to run?"

One day after class Carlos asked Rick, "Why do you run?"

"Because it makes me feel healthy," answered Rick. "Why don't you come with me sometime?"

Carlos didn't know what to say. He didn't really want to go jogging, but he finally said, "OK." Rick told him to bring shorts or sweatpants and some running shoes to school.

The next day after class, the two men changed clothes, and Rick showed Carlos how to do some stretching exercises. Then they started to jog. They ran slowly for about twenty minutes. Then they walked for five minutes. When they finished, Carlos said, "I'm a little tired, but I feel good!"

Now, Carlos jogs with Rick three or four times each week. Sometimes Ana gets a little angry because Carlos comes home later when he jogs. She says, "Running is for rabbits. You need to study, not run." Carlos just shakes his head and smiles.

Comprehension

C. Write *T* before the true sentences and *F* before the false sentences.

____ 1. At first, Carlos didn't understand jogging.
____ 2. Rick likes to be healthy.
____ 3. Carlos didn't really want to jog at first.
____ 4. They ran very quickly the first time.
____ 5. Carlos didn't feel good after they ran.
____ 6. They walked for five minutes after they jogged.
____ 7. Now Ana understands why Carlos wants to jog.

D. Answer these questions about "Running is for Rabbits." Some questions may have more than one answer.

1. Why didn't Carlos want to jog at first?
2. Why does Rick like jogging?
3. Why do they stretch before jogging?
4. Did they run slowly or fast at first? Why?
5. How does Ana feel about jogging? Why do you think she feels that way?

Vocabulary

E. Find the word or phrase on the right that means the same as the word or phrase on the left. Write the correct letter in the blank.

____ 1. sweatshirt, shorts, running shoes
____ 2. jogging
____ 3. angry
____ 4. to stretch
____ 5. to shake your head

a. to reach out far
b. clothes for running
c. mad
d. to turn your head from side to side
e. slow running

Listening

F. Books closed. Try these exercises together in class. Your teacher will read the directions to you.

1. Stand up and reach high with your hands.
2. Touch your toes slowly.
3. Hold your arms out to the side. Make big circles with them. Then make small circles.
4. Breathe in and out slowly three times.

G. Books closed. Your teacher will read the announcement and questions below. Listen carefully and answer the questions about the announcement. Then open your book and check your answers.

There will be a potluck supper for all students in the cafeteria this Friday night at 7:00 p.m. Please bring a friend or your husband or wife. Bring a dish to pass and your own plates, knives, and forks. There will be music and dancing.

1. What night is the potluck?
2. What time is the potluck?
3. Name two things you need to bring to the potluck.
4. Can you bring a friend?
5. What can you do at the potluck?

Now open your book and check your answers.

Conversation

H. Working in pairs, ask each other these questions about free time.

1. Do you have a hobby?
2. What do you do on the weekends?
3. What is your favorite sport?
4. What did you do in your country in your free time? Is it different here?

Your teacher will now make a chart like the one on page 39 using the information about people in your class.

Hobbies	Favorite Sports	What We Did in Our Countries
_____	_____	_____
_____	_____	_____

Writing

I. This story has some mistakes. First, read "Running Is for Rabbits" again. Then, change some of these sentences to make this story true. Finally, copy the correct story.

Example: Rick said, "S~~wimm~~ing makes me feel healthy." *(Jogging)*

Carlos has a Canadian teacher who likes to dance. His name is Fred. The first month of school, Carlos saw Fred dancing down the street in his sweatshirt, sweatpants, and dancing shoes each day after class. Carlos shouted, "Why does he like to dance?"

Reading Practice

J. A picture of a city park is on page 39. Discuss the signs with your classmates, then answer these questions:

1. Can you take a dog to this park?
2. When is it safe to swim? Why?
3. Where will you put trash?
4. Where will you ride a bike?

K. Carlos wrote this story about his favorite hobby, fishing, for his English class. First, talk about the words below. Then read the story.

1. I feel *scared* in the dark.
2. Do you hear that *sound*?
3. There are *rocks* in the lake.
4. Here is my fishing *line*.
5. Don't *lose* the car keys.
6. I feel *proud* when I catch a fish.

FISHING

Carlos Gonzalez

My favorite hobby is fishing. I like to go fishing alone. I like the quiet lake and the sound of the water on the rocks. I can sit and think of many things.

When I feel my line go under the water, I get excited and sometimes a little scared. I don't want to lose the fish. I wait for the right moment and then pull up my line quickly. The fish is strong and beautiful. It fights, but in the end it is mine.

I feel proud when I take my fish home. Sometimes I have many, and sometimes none. I hope I will still be fishing when I am an old man.

Answer these questions about Carlos' story.

1. Why does Carlos like fishing? On the blackboard, make a list of reasons.
2. How does Carlos feel when his line goes under the water? Why?
3. What words does Carlos use to tell about the fish?
4. How does he feel when he takes his fish home?
5. What does Carlos hope?

6

Brrrrr!

Pre-reading

A. What do you think?

1. What is the weather like in your country? Do you have seasons?
2. Have you seen snow or felt very cold weather?
3. Is anyone in the picture warmly dressed?
4. What happens to people in the winter if they are not warmly dressed?

B. What does it mean?

1. In the picture:
   a. Who is wearing a *jacket*?
   b. Is the *wind blowing*? How do you know?
   c. Who is wearing *high heels*?
2. Discuss what these words mean. Then put the correct word into each of the blank spaces.

> hurt   kindness   tears   slippery   late

Kim was (a) _____, so he ran to the bus stop.

He fell down because it was raining and the streets were

(b) _____. He fell on his arm. It (c) _____ a lot.

Kim didn't want to cry, so he held back his (d) _____.

A friend helped him get up. Kim thanked him for his

(e) _____.

Reading

BRRRRR!

It was no fun at the bus stop that cold, gray morning. Everyone was too cold to talk. The bus was late because the streets were filled with snow and ice, and it was very slippery.

Rosa's friend Martha was the coldest. She was wearing a short jacket, a dress, and high heels. She couldn't get warm because of the wind. The blowing snow hurt her face and legs. Her hands were very red, and they hurt. She began to cry a little.

Finally the bus came. Martha walked slowly up the steps. Now her feet hurt, too. An old man saw her tears and cold, red hands. He gave her his big warm mittens to wear until she got off the bus. Martha put them on and then cried a lot! But she was crying because of the old man's kindness.

Martha learned a lot about cold weather that day. After that, she always dressed warmly.

Comprehension

C. Answer these questions about "Brrrrr!"

1. The people at the bus stop didn't talk to each other that morning. Why not?
2. Who was the coldest person waiting for the bus? Why?
3. Who helped Martha get warm?
4. Why did Martha cry?
5. What did Martha learn that morning?

D. Discuss these questions about "Brrrrr!" Some questions have more than one answer.

1. Did you ever meet a kind person like the old man? Did that person help you? How?
2. Why do you think Martha did not dress warmly?

Vocabulary

E. As a group, make a list of weather words. Use these words in sentences. Then put your sentences on the blackboard.

Listening

F. Play a game called "Getting it straight." Everyone has trouble remembering exactly what someone said. Your teacher will tell one person something about the weather. He or she will tell the person next to him. That person will tell the next person, and so on, all around the classroom. The last person will tell the class. See how it changes!

G. Your teacher will read the following letter to you and will put words in the blank spaces to make the letter complete. First listen to the whole letter. Then write the missing words as you hear them.

Dear Mary,

Thanks for your letter. I'm glad everyone in your

(1) _____ is well. We were so (2) _____

to hear from you.

We like the springtime in Madison. It is not as

(3) _____ as winter. The flowers are starting to

(4) _____ and the (5) _____ are singing.

Soon we will (6) _____ our vegetable garden.

I hope you can come and (7) _____ us soon. We

miss (8) _____!

Your friend,

Tina

Writing

H. Now write a letter in English to a friend of yours. Tell your friend about winter or rainy weather where you live. You can copy parts of the letter above.

I. Put these sentences in order. Write them in paragraph form. Start your paragraph with the sentence that has the star.

Martha cried because the old man was so kind.
An old man gave Martha his warm mittens to wear.
*Martha got very cold because she did not wear warm clothes.
After that, Martha always dressed warmly.

Conversation

J. Problem solving. These are problems people have because of the temperature or the weather. What can you do about these problems? Talk about them and write your ideas on the blackboard.

Problem

What to Do

Example: Your apartment is cool. You want to turn up the heat, but it is too expensive.

Dress for the weather. Wear an undershirt, a shirt, and a sweater. (In winter, you will need socks and long underwear.)

1. It's very, very hot outside and you want to play soccer. How can you stay comfortable?

1. _____

_____

_____

2. It's wet or cold outside and your car won't start, so you are late for work sometimes.

2. _____

_____

_____

3. It's very cold and some people in your family don't go outside at all. They start to feel sad.

3. _____

_____

_____

4. Someone in your class doesn't bathe or wash clothes very often. When it's cool, the windows are closed and the room smells bad.

4. _____

_____

_____

Reading Practice

K. Learn about driving in the rain. First, talk about these words with your classmates.

a safe distance   wheel
windshield wipers   to skid

Now read and talk about the list below. Discuss why each idea is important.

DRIVING IN THE RAIN

1. Test your windshield wipers. Be sure you can see well.
2. Slow down on slippery roads.
3. Stay a safe distance behind the car in front of you.
4. Don't stop quickly.
5. If your car skids, turn the wheel in the same direction that you are skidding.
6. In a very heavy rain, get off the road and wait until it is safe to drive.

7

Ana's Nightmare

Pre-reading

A. What do you think?

1. What is a nightmare?
2. Do you usually have happy dreams or nightmares? Do you sometimes have the same dream over and over again?
3. Do you remember one of your dreams? Tell it to your classmates.
4. Do you think dreams tell us something?

B. What does it mean? Can you guess what the italicized words mean?

1. I lived in a *foreign* country last year.
2. The little children put their shoes on *by themselves*.
3. When I listen to English, sometimes I feel *confused*.
4. When I first came to the United States, I thought the food was *strange*. It was very different, and I didn't like it.
5. The parents *wrapped* their baby in a blanket to go outside.
6. After I eat a big meal, I feel sleepy *for a while*. Sometimes I take a little nap.
7. Ana ran down the *aisle* in the grocery store.
8. The winter is *endless* in Wisconsin. It seems very long.

Reading

ANA'S NIGHTMARE

Last night I had a nightmare. I was standing at the entrance of a huge grocery store in a foreign country. I felt confused and nervous. I didn't know what to do. For a while, I watched the glass doors. They were opening and closing by themselves.

The store was very bright, and the lights hurt my eyes. I was hungry, but I didn't understand how to buy anything. The writing on the signs, the cans, and the boxes was strange. The vegetables and fruit were all wrapped in plastic, and the meat was under glass. There was no one to help.

I started to walk down a long aisle. Then the aisle got longer and longer, and I couldn't see the end. At first I walked slowly, then faster. Finally, I was running down the endless aisle and screaming, "Let me out!"

Suddenly, I woke up. I knew it was only a bad dream, so I laughed quietly. I thought about my first days in the United States. Some of those days were like a bad dream.

Comprehension

C. Answer these questions about "Ana's Nightmare."

1. In Ana's dream, where is she? Where is she really?
2. In paragraph 1, find some words that tell how she feels.
3. In paragraph 2, what are three problems Ana had?
4. Why does she run and scream, "Let me out!"?
5. At the end, why does she laugh?

D. Put Ana's story in order by numbering the sentences. Write a 1 in the blank next to the event that happened first, a 2 in the blank next to the event that happened second, etc. The first one is done for you.

___ I started to walk down the aisle.
_1_ I watched the glass doors opening and closing.
___ Suddenly, I woke up.
___ Then the aisle got longer.
___ I was running and screaming.
___ I laughed quietly.

Vocabulary

E. Read the list of words and then write in each blank the word that best completes the sentence.

grocery	vegetables	plastic
signs	fruit	meat

1. Every Saturday, I go to the _____ store to buy some food.

2. I read the _____ at the top of each aisle.

3. I find apples under the _____ sign, carrots under the _____ sign, and beef under the _____ sign.

4. I pay for the food and hope it is all good. I can't touch it because it has _____ around it.

F. Play a tic-tac-toe game with the vocabulary words from exercises B and E. Make a grid on the blackboard and write words in the squares. Divide into two teams. When you explain the meaning of a word, you can mark an *X* or an *O* on that square. When one team wins a game, write new words in the squares and play again.

Listening

G. Books closed. Your teacher will read you a short dream story and will then ask you some questions. Listen carefully, and write the answers to the questions. Open your books to check your answers.

SHORT DREAM STORY

I was up in the air flying. But I wasn't in an airplane—I was flying all by myself! It wasn't scary at all. It felt wonderful. I felt sad after I woke up because I stopped flying. I wanted to sleep again and fly forever.

1. In this dream, where is the person?
2. Is this dream a nightmare?
3. How did the person feel after waking up?

Writing

H. As a class, make up a dream. One person will begin and then each person will say a sentence or two. Your teacher will write the story on the blackboard. Copy it down, and then read it to a partner. Start your story with one of the sentences below if you want to.

I was running faster and faster, but it wasn't fast enough . . .

I saw the ghost walking toward me . . .

I was back in my country . . .

I. For one week, try to remember your dreams when you first wake up in the morning. At the end of the week, choose one of the writing activities below to do as a class or on your own.

1. Write a story about one dream that you had.
2. Write about a dream that you remember from long ago.
3. Make up a dream to write down. Choose a story you would like to have as a dream.

After your teacher corrects your story, read it to the class.

Conversation

J. Think about your first days in the United States. Talk about them with a partner by asking and answering the following questions. Then tell the class one thing about your partner's first days in the United States.

1. How did you come to the United States? How long did the trip take?
2. Who came with you?
3. Were you scared or happy? How did you feel?
4. Did you know any English before you came?
5. What city did you come to first? Where did you live? How did you find a place to live?
6. Did someone help you begin to learn about the United States? Who?
7. What seemed very strange to you at first?
8. Did anything bad happen?
9. Did anything good happen?

Reading Practice

K. Here's a story about Ana's first days in the United States. Read it, answer the questions, and then write a story of your own.

THOSE FIRST DAYS

Ana Gonzalez

Some of those first days in the United States were like a bad dream. I was so tired and so nervous! We had to do a lot, too—find an apartment, buy furniture, buy food, understand important papers—and all in English. I felt funny because Carlos and Rosa knew more English, so they had to do all of these things for me. In our country, I always took care of my children.

Everything was hard. I was homesick. I wanted to see my friends, my family, and my country. We couldn't find the right foods in the grocery store, and we got lost a lot in the city.

It's a lot easier now. We have an apartment and a few friends. We can all go to school, and I have a job.

1. What did Ana, Carlos, and Rosa have to do during those first days in the United States?
2. Did Ana take care of her children? Why or why not?
3. What was Ana homesick for?
4. Is it easier now? Why?

Writing

L. Write a story about your first days in the United States. You can use some of the words from "Those First Days" if you want. The first and last sentences for your story are given below.

Some of those first days in the United States were like a bad dream! _____

_____

_____

_____

_____

_____ But it's easier now!

8

Chocolate Soup

Pre-reading

A. What do you think?

1. Do you like to cook?
2. Who usually cooks in your home?
3. What do you see on the counter in the picture? What do you think Rosa is cooking?
4. Why does the young man in the picture have a funny look on his face?

B. What does it mean? Can you guess what the italicized words mean?

1. The *label* on this can says "Chicken Soup."
2. Can I have your *recipe* for this cake? I want to know how to make it.
3. I make *mistakes* when I speak English.
4. Before I make a cake, I go to the store and buy a *mix*.
5. I like to *taste* different kinds of food. Can I try that soup?
6. Chocolate *fudge* is my favorite candy.

Reading

CHOCOLATE SOUP

Rosa is in the kitchen making fudge when her friend Dan comes in. Rosa makes a big mistake! Can you guess what she does wrong?

Dan: Hey Rosa! What are you making? It looks like chocolate soup.

Rosa: It's fudge. Do you want to taste it?

Dan: I don't know. Is it good?

Rosa: It's great! My friend made it for me last week and I loved it. I'm using her recipe now. Go ahead and try it.

Dan: Yuk! This is terrible!

Rosa: You're kidding. What's wrong?

Dan: It's too salty.

Rosa: Salty? There's no salt in the recipe . . . just sugar, butter, milk, and chocolate.

Dan: Well, let's look at what you put in the fudge. Here's the chocolate, butter, milk, and . . . Rosa! Read this label! It's salt, not sugar.

Rosa: Oh, no! You're right! I forgot to read the label. We can't eat this.

Dan: That's OK. We can start over. But this time, let's go to the store and buy a box of fudge mix.

Rosa: Good idea. Let's go.

Comprehension

C. Write *T* before the true sentences and *F* before the false sentences.

____ 1. Rosa reads labels carefully when she cooks.
____ 2. Rosa is using her friend's fudge recipe.
____ 3. Rosa makes a mistake with sugar and salt.
____ 4. Dan thinks the fudge is great.
____ 5. Rosa and Dan will buy a fudge mix and start over.

D. Answer these questions about the dialogue.

1. What does Dan think Rosa is making?
2. What things does Rosa put in the fudge?
3. Why does the fudge taste bad?

Vocabulary

E. Find the phrase on the right that means the same as the word on the left. Write the correct letter in the blank.

____ 1. recipe
____ 2. fudge
____ 3. to taste
____ 4. label
____ 5. a mix

a. to try a small bite of food
b. words on the outside of a box that tell you what is inside
c. directions for cooking
d. chocolate candy
e. cake or fudge that you can make fast from a box

F. As a group, find the following expressions in "Chocolate Soup." Talk about *when* you say these expressions.

start over   Go ahead
try it   What's wrong?
You're kidding!

Now use the expressions to fill in the blanks below.

1. You look nervous today. _____ _____?

2. This fudge is terrible. Let's buy a mix and _____ _____ again.

3. This is a fruit salad. Please _____ _____. I think you'll like it.

4. *Carlos:* I got an A on my math test.

   Rosa: _____ _____! I can't believe it!

5. *Students:* Can we begin the test now?

   Teacher: Sure. _____ _____ and start.

Listening

G. Your teacher will read the first four lines of "Chocolate Soup." Listen carefully and write the sentences on the lines below.

Dan: _____

_____

Rosa: _____

_____

Dan: _____

_____

Rosa: _____

_____

Now read the sentences back to your teacher who will write them on the blackboard. Then practice reading.

Conversation

H. Work in groups of three. Ask two classmates these questions about food. Then, as a whole class, talk about your answers.

1. What is an American food you like?
2. What is an American food you don't like?
3. What food can you cook well?
4. What food from your country do you miss?

I. Talk about holidays in your country. Think about the questions below. Then give a little speech to your class with your answers.

1. What is your favorite holiday in your country?
2. What are the special foods for that holiday?
3. What do people usually do on that day?

Example: My favorite holiday is Thanksgiving. The special foods for that day are turkey and pumpkin pie. On Thanksgiving Day we have a big meal with our friends and family.

Writing

J. Copy this story and make the story true for you. Your teacher can spell words for you.

EATING!

In my country, we eat (1) _____ meals a day. In the morning we eat (2) _____ and (3) _____.

Our biggest meal is at (4) _____ p.m. Then we usually

eat (5) _____ and (6) _____ and (7)

_____. (8) _____ cooks the meals in my

family. (9) _____ helps clean the kitchen after the

meal.

Now read your story to your classmates.

Reading Practice

K. This is a recipe for chocolate-peanut candy. First, talk about the words below. Some of them are *abbreviations*. Then read the recipe and answer the questions. You can try the recipe at home or at school.

melt	teaspoon
lb.	pkg.
oz.	stir

CHOCOLATE-PEANUT CANDY

1 lb. white chocolate
1 6 oz. pkg. semi-sweet chocolate chips
1 6 oz. pkg. milk chocolate chips
1 12 oz. jar dry roasted peanuts

DIRECTIONS
1. Melt chocolate in a pan on low heat. Stir often.
2. Let cool 5 minutes.
3. Add peanuts and stir.
4. Drop by teaspoons onto waxed paper.
5. Cool. Keep in refrigerator.
Makes about 30 pieces of candy.

Answer these questions about the recipe.

1. How many kinds of chocolate do you use?
2. How much white chocolate do you need?
3. How many ounces of peanuts do you need?
4. When do you stir in the peanuts?
5. How many pieces of candy will the recipe make?
6. Where do you keep the candy when you are finished?

9

Grandpa's Here!

Pre-reading

A. What do you think?

1. Do you think traveling is fun? Difficult? Are you afraid to travel?
2. How do people feel when they come to the United States for the first time?
3. What are some problems you can have when you travel by plane? By car?

B. What does it mean? Find a sentence on the right that means the same as a sentence on the left. Write the correct letter in the blank.

___ 1. They *met* Grandpa at the airport.

___ 2. He lives *outside* the United States.

___ 3. The *airport* is huge.

___ 4. They *got lost*.

___ 5. There are many different *sounds* in a city.

a. He does not live in the United States.

b. They didn't know where they were.

c. They went to the airport to pick up Grandpa.

d. A city is full of noise—cars, people, horns, etc.

e. The airport is very large.

Reading

Grandpa is coming to the United States. Do you think he'll like it?

GRANDPA'S HERE!

November 1 was a big day. Ana, Carlos, and Rosa drove to the airport in Chicago to meet Grandpa. Carlos borrowed his friend Dan's car for the trip. It was the first time Carlos drove outside of Madison and the family's first visit to Chicago. Carlos didn't know the way, but he took a map.

Near the airport, Carlos, Rosa, and Ana got lost. They took the wrong road and started to drive back to Madison. Rosa was reading the road signs. Suddenly she said, "Carlos! Did you see that sign? It said, 'Madison, 85 miles.' We're going in the wrong direction!"

Carlos stopped at a gas station and asked for directions. He had to stop and ask for help two more times, but they finally arrived at the airport. Now they had to find Grandpa's plane.

The Chicago airport is huge. They had to follow the signs carefully to find the right gate. When they got there, the passengers were coming out of the plane. Finally a small man with a bag full of presents walked through the door. It was Grandpa! Carlos, Rosa, and Ana ran to him with tears and smiles.

It was an easy drive back to Madison—no problems this time. Everyone went to bed early, but poor Grandpa didn't sleep well. He was listening to all the new sounds and thinking about all the strange things he saw that day. It was so different from Central America!

Comprehension

C. Answer these questions about "Grandpa's Here!"

1. How did Grandpa get to Chicago?
2. Who went to meet him in Chicago? What happened on the way to the airport?
3. How did Carlos and his family get help?
4. How do you know everyone was happy to see Grandpa?
5. Grandpa didn't sleep well. Why not?

Vocabulary

D. Put each of these words in one of the blank spaces.

> directions   get lost
> outside   meet

Grandpa is happy that he came to Madison. He has never been (1) _____ his country before, and he is very interested in everything. Grandpa likes to (2) _____ new people and visit new places. He is not afraid to ask for (3) _____, so he doesn't (4) _____ very often.

E. Discuss these words and expressions. Practice using them in sentences. Write your sentences on the blackboard.

Words	*Expressions*
1. suddenly	a. to get lost
2. presents	b. to ask for directions
3. (airport) gate	c. to worry about
4. tears	d. to go the wrong way
5. huge	e. to be a big day
6. borrow	f. a long distance

Listening

F. Books closed. Listen to these directions to the airport. You will hear them two times. Then answer the questions about them on a piece of paper.

1. Go straight for three miles.
2. When you get to First Street, turn right.
3. The airport is on First Street. You'll see it on your left.

Questions:

1. What street do you turn on? Which way?
2. What street is the airport on?

Now you want to go to the bus station. You stop and ask for directions again. Listen and then answer the questions on a piece of paper.

1. You are now on Lake Street.
2. Go to the next corner and turn left. Then you will be on Third Street.
3. You'll see the bus station after three blocks.

Questions:

1. Is the bus station on Lake Street?
2. Do you turn right or left on Third Street?
3. How far do you go on Third Street?

Writing

G. Read the first paragraph of the story again. Then write the first paragraph as the teacher reads it to you.

_____

_____

_____

_____

Now look in your book and correct your paragraph.

H. Write about your first car trip in the United States.

Our first trip to _____ was fun but tiring. We had some problems. First, _____

_____ .

Then, _____

_____ .

But we really enjoyed the trip because _____

_____ .

Conversation

I. Working with a partner, practice giving directions to places in your school or in your community.

Directions

1. From the office to your classroom
2. From the front door to the library
3. From the library to your classroom
4. From your classroom to the bus stop
5. From your school to the post office

Helpful expressions

a. Turn right (left)
b. At the corner
c. Go straight until . . .
d. It's near the . . .
e. It's across from . . .

J. These are problems people have when they travel. What can you do about the problems? Talk about them and write your ideas on the blackboard.

Problem

Example: a lost suitcase

What to Do

Go to the lost and found.
Go to the ticket counter.

1. Your plane will be late to arrive. You worry because people are waiting for you or you need to change planes.

1. _____
_____
_____

2. You arrive in a strange city and no one meets you.

2. _____
_____

3. You are in a strange city and you get lost.

3. _____
_____

4. You need help at the airport, but people can't understand you.

4. _____
_____

Problem

5. You are traveling by bus. You need help because you are not sure when to get off the bus.

What to Do

5. _____

_____

_____

_____

Reading Practice

K. This is a road map. It shows the roads between Madison and Chicago. Look at the map with your classmates and answer the questions on page 68.

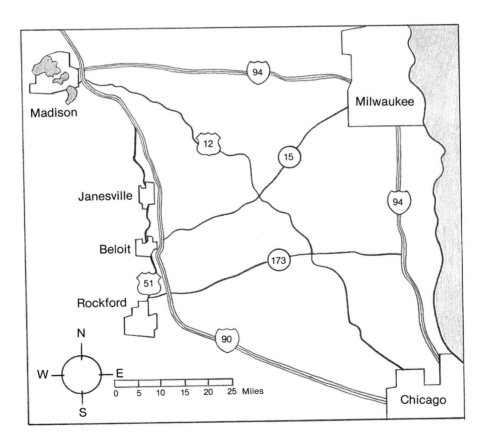

1. Find north, south, east, and west on the map. If you are in Madison, where is Chicago (to the north or to the south)? If you are in Chicago, where is Madison (north or south)?
2. What is the number of the highway from Madison to Chicago?
3. How does the map tell you this is an important road?
4. Name some large towns near this highway.
5. How far is it from Madison to Chicago?
6. How long do you think it takes to drive from Madison to Chicago?

10

Mom Doesn't Understand

Pre-reading

A. What do you think?

1. It's a Tuesday night and it is very late. Why do you think Ana and Grandpa are waiting for Carlos?
2. Ana isn't very happy. What do you think the problem is?

B. What does it mean? Can you guess what the italicized words mean?

1. Carlos and his *girlfriend* like to *go out* on Saturday night.
2. You can drink beer or wine in a *bar*.
3. My friend will *make her own decision* to come to the United States.
4. Please don't *stay out* late. Come home at 10:00.

Reading

MOM DOESN'T UNDERSTAND

Ana: Carlos, we need to talk. Grandpa and I are worried about you. You go out every night after dinner and we don't see you much anymore. What do you do?

Carlos: Mom, I'm twenty years old. I'm an adult now and I can make my own decisions. Everything's fine.

Ana: No, it isn't. You need more sleep. Do you have a girlfriend? Do you go to bars?

Carlos: Mom, no more questions. It's late and I'm tired. Let's talk tomorrow.

Grandpa: Carlos, answer your mother's questions.

Carlos: OK. I *do* have a girlfriend. Her name is Sally Baker. We study together and we like to go out, too.

Ana: But you stay out so late. What about her family?

Carlos: She doesn't live at home. She has an apartment.

Ana: An apartment? For a young girl? I can't believe it!

Grandpa: Things are really different here in the United States.

Ana: Yes, they are. I'm trying to understand.

Carlos:	Mom, I'm doing fine. Don't worry about me. Now, good night, Grandpa. Good night, Mom.
Ana and Grandpa:	Good night, Carlos.

Comprehension

C. Write *T* for the true sentences and *F* for the false ones.

____ 1. Ana and Grandpa think everything is fine.
____ 2. Ana and Grandpa want to talk with Carlos.
____ 3. Carlos wants Mom's help.
____ 4. For young people, life in the United States is the same as life in other countries.
____ 5. Ana is trying to understand Carlos.

D. Answer these questions. The questions may have more than one answer.

1. Why do Ana and Grandpa want to talk to Carlos?
2. Name three things Ana worries about.
3. Is Carlos worried about himself? Why or why not?
4. Sally doesn't live at home. Why?
5. Explain the sentence, "I can make my own decisions."

Vocabulary

E. Find the phrase on the right that means the same as the phrase on the left. Write the correct letter in the blank.

____ 1. I can make my own decisions.
____ 2. I'm going out with someone tonight.
____ 3. Things are different here.
____ 4. Everything's fine.
____ 5. I can't believe it!

a. I don't understand; I don't think it's right.
b. There's no problem.
c. I have a date tonight.
d. Life is not the same here.
e. I can decide by myself.

Conversation

F. Think and talk about these questions.

1. When do children become adults? At what age can children make their own decisions?
2. When can young people go out alone on a date in your country?
3. In your country, what happens when parents tell their children to do something and the children say, "No!"?
4. In the United States, many people think it is important for families to talk about family problems. Is it the same in your culture?
5. Do parents' ideas change when they move to a new country? How about children's ideas?

Listening

G. Books closed. Your teacher will read this story about Grandpa to you. Listen carefully. You will be asked to write three things about Grandpa.

My Grandpa is seventy-six years old. He is short and a little fat, and he doesn't have much hair. Grandpa is kind and gentle, and he always listens to me carefully. Grandpa is a very special person for me.

Now, on a piece of paper, write three things about Grandpa. Then open your book and check your answers.

Writing

H. Write four things about someone who is special for *you*. Use these questions and the story about Grandpa to help you write your sentences.

1. Who is the person and how old is he or she?
2. What does the person look like?
3. What are some special things that this person does?
4. How do you feel about this person?

Reading Practice

I. Many U.S. newspapers have one writer who answers letters from people who have problems. Below you will find one of these letters and its answer. Read and talk about the letters. Answer the questions.

Dear Ms. Helpful: I am thirteen years old and I am very unhappy. I really like a boy who is in my class at school. He likes me, too! But that's not why I am unhappy.

This boy asked me to go to a movie with him. We made plans to go, but then my mom said I was too young to date. I cried and cried, but she won't change her ideas! Ms. Helpful, what can I do? Thirteen is old enough to date and too young to be so unhappy.

— Sadly, Amy

Dear Amy: I think you have a problem, but I think you are lucky, too. It's nice that this boy likes you! It's also nice that your mom loves you so much. She said "No" because she loves you and worries about you.

Now here is an answer to your problem. Maybe your mom thinks you are too young because you cried and cried. Try to talk to her without crying. Try to show her in other ways that you are old enough to go out on a date. For example, make sure that your grades in school are good!

If your mom still says "No," you can still go to the movie. Ask two girls and two boys to go with you and *all* of you can have a good time.

— Good Luck! Ms. Helpful

Answer these questions about the letters.

1. Who is Ms. Helpful? Can you find someone like her in a real newspaper?
2. Why is Amy unhappy?
3. Do you think Amy is old enough to date? Why or why not?
4. What does Ms. Helpful tell Amy about Mom? Do you think she is right?
5. What three ideas does Ms. Helpful have for Amy to try?

Writing

J. As a class, write a letter to Ms. Helpful from Amy's mom. What will she say about Amy and dating? Begin your letter like this:

Dear Ms. Helpful,

I'm having a problem with my daughter, Amy. _____

_____

_____

_____

_____

                                    Sincerely,
                                    Mom

11

Crash!

Pre-reading

A. What do you think?

1. What is an accident?
2. Have you ever had a car accident?
3. What is car insurance? Why is it important?

B. What does it mean? Talk about these words with your classmates. Then find these in the pictures below.

intersection	ticket
police officer	crash
police report	

Reading

CRASH!

1. Rosa is driving her friend Martha's car to the airport. Martha is flying home from Chicago, and Rosa is going to pick her up. Rosa is being very careful because it's not her car.

Rosa is coming to an intersection, but she doesn't have to stop. Another car is coming, but that driver has to stop because there's a stop sign.

2. CRASH! The other driver didn't stop at the stop sign. Nobody is hurt but Rosa is angry! "Why didn't you stop? You had a stop sign, you know!" says Rosa.

"I'm really sorry," says the other driver. "I didn't see the stop sign. It's my fault. I'll go call the police."

3. The police officer writes a police report. She talks to Rosa and the other driver, whose name is Paul Werner. She gives a ticket to Paul because he didn't stop at the stop sign.

It will cost a lot to fix Martha's car. Luckily, Paul has good insurance. His insurance will pay for most of the damage because the accident was his fault.

4. Paul called Rosa to give her some insurance information. They talked for a long time. They decided to meet for coffee to look at the insurance papers. Rosa said, "I'll meet you at 10:00 tomorrow, and please remember . . . stop at all the stop signs on the way!"

Comprehension

C. Answer these questions about the story.

1. Whose car was Rosa driving? Why?
2. What happened at the intersection?
3. Did they call an ambulance? Why or why not?
4. Who got a ticket?
5. Who will pay to fix Martha's car?

D. Answer these questions about "CRASH!" The questions may have more than one answer.

1. What do you think Martha will say about the accident?
2. Is Rosa still angry at Paul?
3. What problems can you have when you borrow someone's car?

Vocabulary

E. Read and discuss these words. Then write in each blank the word that best completes the sentence.

insurance company	nobody	luckily
damage	hurt	information
fault	pick up	

1. Paul got a ticket because the accident was his _____.

2. The _____ will pay to fix Martha's car.

3. No ambulance came because Rosa and Paul were not _____.

4. It will cost $400.00 to fix the _____ on Martha's car.

5. _____ was hurt.

6. I have to _____ _____ the children at school at 12:00. They will be waiting for me.

7. I saw a car accident yesterday. _____ no one was hurt.

8. I need your name, address, and phone number. Please write that _____ on this paper for me.

Listening

F. Read the story again and think about the accident. Then tell a classmate the story in your own words. Your classmate will listen carefully to make sure you tell everything in order. Then your classmate will tell the story and you will listen carefully.

G. Books closed. Your teacher will read the following weather report two or three times. First, talk about *fog*, then listen carefully and get ready to answer some questions about the report. After you answer the questions, open your book and check your answers.

There is heavy fog in the Madison area this morning. Cars are moving slowly on the highways, and driving is dangerous. Buses are about ten to fifteen minutes late. If you are driving to work, you should leave a few minutes early. Drive carefully!

1. What is the weather in Madison today?
2. Why are cars moving slowly?
3. How late are the buses?
4. When should you leave for work this morning?

Conversation

H. Rosa and Martha are very good friends. They met each other at school. Can you and your classmates think of some other ways to make friends here in the United States? Can you tell about how you made a friend here? Your teacher will write your ideas on the blackboard. Add to this list:

How to Make Friends

1. Go to community classes.
2. Talk to neighbors.

3. _____

4. _____

I. An accident is something that can make you feel *scared* or *frightened*. With your classmates, talk about a time that you felt scared or frightened. Each student can finish this sentence:

I felt scared when _____.

Ask the person questions about his or her frightening experience.

Writing

J. Practice making some emergency phone calls with your classmates. With a partner, read the conversations below and fill in the blanks with information about you. Then read your conversations to your classmates.

1. You had a car accident and you need to report it, so call the police. Nobody was hurt.

   a. Hello, police? I want to report a car accident.

   Police: Where?

   a. _____

   Police: Is anyone hurt?

   a. _____

   Police: What's your name?

   a. _____

   Police: A police officer will be there quickly.

2. You had a car accident and someone is hurt. Call for an ambulance.

   Ambulance driver: Hello, this is Emergency Medical Service.

   b. We need an ambulance right away because somebody is hurt.

   _____

   Ambulance driver: Where are you?

   b. _____

   Ambulance driver: What is your name?

   b. _____

   Ambulance driver: We're on the way.

Reading Practice

K. This list tells you what to do if you have a car accident. With your classmates, read and talk about why each idea is important. Then try to remember what you will do first, second, third, and so on.

If You Have a Car Accident . . .

1. Watch out for more cars coming.
2. Call an ambulance if people are hurt.
   a. Don't move the person who is hurt.
   b. If the person is bleeding, try to stop it.
   c. Keep the person warm.
   d. Don't let the person's head move around.
3. Call police or ask someone to call for you.
4. Write down the name, address, phone number, car license number, and insurance company of the other driver.
5. Call your insurance company soon.

L. Read the list above one more time. Then put the following list in order (write 1 for the first step, 2 for the second, etc.). Don't look back. The first one is done for you.

____ Help people who are hurt.
____ Call your insurance company.
____ Call the police.
_1_ Watch out for more cars.
____ Call the ambulance if needed.
____ Write down the name, address, phone number, license number, and insurance company of the other driver.

Now check your answers with the list above.

M. Read the problem below. Talk about the problem with your classmates and make a list of things to do on the blackboard.

PROBLEM: You just had a car accident and someone is hurt. You called an ambulance. Now you are waiting for the ambulance to come. What can you do to help the person who is hurt?

Now look again at exercise K, number 2, to check your list.

12

Ice Cream or Apples?

Pre-reading

A. What do you think?

1. Look at Rosa. What is she trying to do?
2. Did you *gain weight* when you came to this country? Why do some people gain weight when they first come to the United States?

3. Think about the foods you ate in your country and the foods you eat in the United States. Are they the same or different? How?
4. Why do so many Americans want to be *thin*?
5. Name the foods pictured around the reading "Ice Cream or Apples?"

B. What does it mean? Read and discuss the list of words. Then write in each blank the word or phrase that best completes the sentence.

to gain weight	meal
fattening	snack
go on a diet	to fit

1. Many people feel hungry just before they go to bed, so they eat a
   snack   .

2. In the United States, most people eat a big _____ in the evening.

3. Some people are too thin. They need _____.

4. Rosa's skirt is too tight. She's not happy because she wants it _____ her.

5. Some people are too fat. They want to lose weight, so they

   _____.

6. Cookies, ice cream, and candy are _____ foods.

Reading

ICE CREAM OR APPLES?

Rosa: Mama! Look at this skirt! It doesn't fit! It's too tight. I'm gaining so much weight.

Ana: You look fine, Rosa.

Rosa: No I don't! I want to be thin. I'm going on a diet tomorrow.

Ana: You don't need to go on a diet. Just eat three good meals a day and not so many fattening snacks!

Rosa: But I love snacks like soda pop, candy bars, potato chips . . .

Ana: Yes, but those foods aren't good for you. You gain weight when you eat a lot of those things because they have so much fat and sugar in them.

Rosa: But what about the bag of potato chips I just bought?

Carlos: I'll worry about the potato chips.

Rosa: I'm sure you will!

Comprehension

C. Answer these questions about "Ice Cream or Apples?"

1. Why does Rosa want to go on a diet?
2. Does Ana think Rosa is too fat?
3. What does Ana tell Rosa about eating? Do you agree?
4. Who will eat the potato chips?
5. The word *fat* means something different in these two sentences. Discuss the different meanings:
   a. I'm getting too fat!
   b. There's a lot of fat in potato chips.

D. Write *T* before the true sentences and *F* before the false sentences.

____ 1. Rosa's skirt doesn't fit.
____ 2. Rosa thinks she is too fat, so she will go on a diet.
____ 3. Ana thinks Rosa is too fat.
____ 4. Rosa likes fattening snacks.
____ 5. Candy bars and soda are good for you.

Vocabulary

E. Look at the two sentences. If the sentences mean the same, circle *S*. If they are different, circle *D*.

1. Anita is too *thin*.   S Ⓓ
   Anita is too *fat*.
2. Candy bars are a *fattening* food.   S D
   Candy bars are good for you.
3. Mrs. Mett is *gaining weight*.   S D
   Mrs. Mett is getting fatter.
4. These jeans are too *tight*.   S D
   These jeans are too small.
5. Let's have a *snack*!   S D
   Let's have dinner!

F. Which foods have a lot of fat and/or sugar? Add some to the following list:

Foods with a Lot of Fat and/or Sugar

a. candy bars
b. margarine or butter
c. french fries
d.
e.
f.
g.

Listening

G. Your teacher will read the dialogue again to you. Write the lines that are missing.

Rosa: Mama! Look at this skirt! It doesn't fit! It's too tight! I'm gaining so much weight.

Ana: _____

Rosa: No, I don't. I want to be thin. I'm going on a diet tomorrow.

Ana: _____

Rosa: But I love snacks like soda pop, candy bars, potato chips . . .

Ana: _____
_____
_____

Rosa: But what about the bag of potato chips I just bought?

Carlos: _____

Rosa: I'm sure you will!

Conversation

1. Eat four foods from the bread-cereal group.

2. Eat four foods from the fruit-vegetable group.

3. Eat two foods from the meat group.

4. Adults should eat two or more servings.
   Teenagers should eat four or more servings.

H. Read the sentences under the pictures on page 86.

1. Make lists of all the foods in each picture.
2. Add other foods to each food group. How many can you think of? Write your lists on the blackboard and copy the lists to use later.

I. Your teacher will read the names of foods below. Make two lists on your paper. Label one "Good for you" and the other "Not so good for you." Write each food in one of the lists. One student can write on the board. Talk about your lists when you finish.

Example: *Good for you*   *Not so good for you*

apples   chocolate candy

_____   _____

_____   _____

Foods

1. rice
2. carrots
3. french fries
4. candy bars
5. beef
6. sweet rolls
7. milk
8. soda pop
9. bananas
10. noodles
11. fish
12. chocolate cookies

J. Think about the foods you eat each day. Then, discuss the questions below.

1. Do you eat foods from each of the food groups each day?
2. Do you eat breakfast every day?
3. Do you eat snacks that are good for you?
4. Do you eat different kinds of foods?
5. How can you make your diet better?

K. Rosa is planning the menus for her family for one week. This is her plan for Monday. What do you think of her menu? As you discuss the menu, think about the picture above exercise H and these questions:

1. Are there four fruits or vegetables?
2. Are there two foods from the meat group?
3. Are there two foods from the milk group?
4. Are there four foods from the bread-cereal group?
5. Are there too many foods that have a lot of fat or sugar?
6. Can you make the menu better? How?

Breakfast	*Lunch*	*Supper*
milk	chicken sandwich	beef
doughnut	rice soup	rice
coffee	apple	green beans
	soda pop	milk
		cookies

Now work as a class to plan a one-day menu for Rosa and her family. Choose healthful foods that you like. Use the food lists you made in exercise H, above. When you finish, answer the questions (1–6, above) about your menu.

Breakfast   *Lunch*   *Supper*

_____   _____   _____

_____   _____   _____

Are you ready to plan a one-day menu all by yourself? Try it and then discuss it with a partner by asking each other the questions again (1–6, above).

Breakfast   *Lunch*   *Supper*

_____   _____   _____

_____   _____   _____

Writing

L. Work with a partner to complete the dialogue below. Rosa is telling her friend Martha how to eat better. Read your dialogue to the class when you finish.

Martha: Oh, I'm always so tired at 10:00 in the morning.

Rosa: Do you eat breakfast?

Martha: No, _____

Rosa: You won't be so tired every morning if you eat breakfast.

Martha: _____

Rosa: _____

Reading Practice

M. It is important to read labels when you buy food at the grocery store. Read the labels below, talk about what important information they tell you, and answer the questions.

1.
MILK
Buy before
October 18

2.
BABY FOOD
Expiration date:
April 3 1989

3.
FRUIT DRINK
No sugar

1. Will this milk be OK to drink on November 3?
2. Can you give this food to a baby in June 1989?
3. Is this fruit drink fattening?

13

Just Married

Pre-reading

A. What do you think?

1. With your classmates, share what you know about American weddings.
2. Where can Americans have a wedding?

B. What does it mean?

1. Can you find each of these new words in the picture above?

a. groom   c. bride   e. church
b. balloon   d. to wave

2. As a class, discuss what these words mean. Then choose the best word for each of the blank spaces.

reception   congratulated
decorated   got married
relatives   guests
wedding

a. Dan and Helen _____ in a church.

b. The _____ was beautiful. The family _____ the church with flowers.

c. Dan's uncles, aunts, grandparents — all of his _____ came to the wedding.

d. After the wedding in the church, everyone went to the _____. There they _____ the bride and groom.

e. When Dan and Helen left the reception, all the _____ went outside to wave good-bye.

Reading

JUST MARRIED

Dan got married on a warm Saturday afternoon in the spring. He and his bride, Helen, had a big church wedding. Their friends and relatives came from near and far to help them celebrate. Carlos, Ana, Rosa, and Grandpa went to both the wedding and the wedding reception which was in the basement of the church. They thought the wedding was beautiful, but Grandpa got a little sleepy. Ana and Rosa loved the beautiful dresses and the flowers. Carlos thought the wedding was nice, but he liked the reception better.

At the reception, Carlos first congratulated the bride and groom. Then he looked for some of his friends. Everyone danced, ate, and talked to friends. It was a good party.

Later, when it was almost time for the bride and groom to leave the reception, Carlos and his friends went outside and decorated Dan's car. They put signs on it. One sign said, "Honk your horn. We just got married!" Carlos also tied balloons and tin cans to the back of the car.

When all the guests went outside to wave good-bye to the bride and groom, they saw Dan's car with the funny signs, balloons, and tin cans. Everyone thought it looked great. Carlos was glad. He wanted the car to be really nice for Dan and Helen.

Comprehension

C. Answer the questions about "Just Married."

1. Where was the wedding ceremony?
2. Who came to the wedding?
3. Where did everyone go after the wedding ceremony?
4. Name three things people do at a wedding reception.
5. How did Carlos and his friends decorate Dan's car?

Vocabulary

D. Discuss the meanings of the italicized words. After reading the sentences, put them in the correct order.

1. At the reception, everyone first *congratulated* the bride and groom.
2. The *guests* waited in the church for the wedding to begin.
3. During the reception, Dan's friends *decorated* his car.

4. The bride and groom *got married*. Then everyone went to the *reception*.

5. Finally, the guests *waved* as the bride and groom drove away.

Conversation

E. Talk about weddings in other cultures with your classmates. Compare how weddings are the same and different in three or four cultures. As a class, complete the chart below. Think of some more questions to add to the chart.

Question	Culture U.S.	Culture	Culture
How old are people when they marry?	18+		
Who chooses the bride (or groom)?	They choose each other.		
Who pays for the wedding?	Parents of bride, or bride and groom, or parents of both.		
What clothes do the bride and groom wear?	Long white dress Tuxedo		
What kind of wedding party do they have?	A reception in a church, hotel, or restaurant.		
What kinds of presents do people give?	Useful things for a home, or money.		
Where do the bride and groom live after the wedding?	In their own apartment.		

F. A wedding reception is one kind of party. Another kind of party is a New Year's party. Listen to your classmates tell about New Year's parties in their culture.

1. What kind of party is it?
2. Who comes to the party?
3. Where is the party?

When each person finishes, be ready to tell three things that they said.

Listening

G. Books closed. Your teacher will read these two problems to you. You will hear them two times. Then answer the questions about them on a piece of paper. After you answer the questions, open your book and check your answers.

1. Tom is thirty-eight years old and Mary is thirty-five. They have been married for five years. Tom wants Mary to stop work and have children. Mary likes her job and wants to do well in her work. Mary thinks she can't have children now because she does not have a lot of extra time.

Questions

a. How old is Tom?
b. Does Mary want to stop working?
c. Who wants children now?

Discuss what you think Tom and Mary will do.

2. Pablo and Lidia are eighteen years old. They will graduate from high school next year. They both have part-time jobs, but they don't earn much money. Lidia wants to stop working, get married, and start a family.

Questions

a. How old are Pablo and Lidia?
b. Does Lidia have a job?
c. Does Pablo earn a lot of money?

Discuss what you think Pablo and Lidia will do.

Writing

H. Ana's neighbor Tina gave her a sweater for her birthday. Help Ana write a thank you note to Tina.

Dear Tina,

Thank you so much for _____. It is very

_____. I will wear _____.

_____

_____

Your friend,

Ana

I. Yesterday you got a _____ for your birthday. Now you have to write a thank you note.

_____

_____

_____

_____

Reading Practice

J. Read this story about a surprise party for Carlos. First discuss these words and phrases:

birthday party   birthday cake
to be ready   presents
hiding place

HAPPY BIRTHDAY!

It's a good thing Carlos likes parties because his girlfriend, Sally, is having a surprise birthday party for him. Carlos thinks that he and Sally are going to the movies at 7:00. But they aren't.

Carlos will come to Sally's apartment to pick her up. Sally will open the door and say, "Hi, Carlos. Please come in for a minute. I'm not ready yet." When Carlos steps into the living room, all of his friends from school will come out from their hiding places and shout, "Happy Birthday!"

They all have funny presents for Carlos. Sally is going to give him a toy car because Carlos is always talking about getting a car. Carlos will have a birthday cake, and there will be singing and dancing to records. Carlos will love it!

Answer these questions about "Happy Birthday!"

1. What is a surprise party?
2. Where does Carlos think he is going with Sally?
3. What kind of presents will Carlos get? Why?
4. Do you think a surprise party is a good idea? Why or why not?

14

Is It Broken?

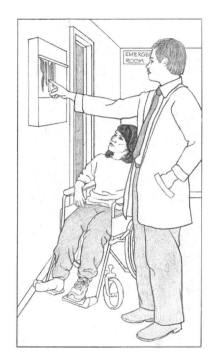

Pre-reading

A. What do you think?

1. Why is Rosa in the wheelchair? Where is she? Why do you think she is there?
2. Who is your family doctor? Which hospital will you go to if you have an accident? (If you don't know, ask someone at home.)

3. What is health insurance? Why do you need it? How do you get it?

4. Have you been to a hospital in this country? What was it like?

B. What does it mean?

1. Say these words after your teacher. Then talk about what they mean. The picture will help you understand them.

> emergency room   X ray
> wheelchair   ankle

2. Can you guess the meaning of the italicized words?

I fell down this morning and *sprained* my ankle. Now I can't walk. I went to the emergency room, and the doctor took an *X ray* of my ankle. Then she looked at the picture and said, "It's not *broken*."

My ankle hurts! I'm *in a lot of pain*. The doctor gave me a *prescription* for some pain medicine.

I have to go to the drugstore and get it.

Reading

IS IT BROKEN?

After school one day, Rosa hurt her ankle during a volleyball game. She was in a lot of pain and didn't know what to do. Her friends decided to call her doctor. Luckily, Rosa knew his name. The doctor told them to go to the emergency room at Madison Hospital. Before they left for the hospital, Rosa's friends called her mom. Ana said, "Grandpa and I will meet you at the emergency room right away."

At the hospital emergency room, a nurse brought a wheelchair for Rosa. Then the nurse asked Rosa to fill out insurance papers. Rosa didn't know anything about insurance, and she didn't want to think about it. She was still in a lot of pain! Just then, Ana and Grandpa came, so Ana began to fill out the papers.

Grandpa went with Rosa to a small room to wait for a doctor. The doctor came, took an X ray, and then showed Rosa the picture of her ankle. She had a sprained ankle, not a broken one. The doctor told Rosa to rest and put ice on her ankle, and gave her a prescription for some pain medicine.

When they left, Ana said, "We're lucky for two reasons. Your ankle isn't broken and the insurance will pay for everything." Rosa didn't feel so lucky; she just felt pain!

Comprehension

C. Write *T* before the true sentences and *F* before the false sentences.

____ 1. Rosa's ankle hurt a little.
____ 2. Rosa knew her family doctor's name.
____ 3. Rosa knew the insurance information.
____ 4. Rosa's friends took her to the doctor's office.
____ 5. Rosa's ankle was broken.
____ 6. Rosa and her family have to pay for everything.

D. Read the sentences below. Put them in order by writing a 1 before the event that happened first, a 2 before the event that happened second, and so on. The first one is done for you.

____ Ana filled out the insurance papers.
_1_ Rosa hurt her ankle playing volleyball.
____ Rosa and Grandpa waited for the doctor.
____ The X ray showed that Rosa had a sprained ankle.
____ Rosa's doctor said, "Go to the emergency room."
____ Rosa went home to rest.

E. Answer the following questions. The answers may not be in "Is It Broken?"

1. The hospital wanted Rosa's insurance information. Why?
2. How did the doctor know Rosa's ankle wasn't broken?
3. What should you do for a sprained ankle?
4. When should you go to the emergency room? When should you go to the doctor's office?

Vocabulary

F. Read and discuss these words. Then write in each blank the word that best completes the sentence.

X ray   wheelchair
prescription   sprained
emergency room broken
ankle

Carlos was playing soccer and hurt his (1) _____ .

He went to the (2) _____ at the hospital. He sat in a

(3) _____ because he couldn't walk. They took an

(4) _____ of his ankle. He was lucky! It wasn't

(5) _____ . But his ankle was (6) _____ ,

and he was in a lot of pain. So the doctor gave him a

(7) _____ for some pain medicine.

Listening

G. Your teacher will read the following paragraph from "Is It Broken?" two times. The first time just listen. The second time fill in the missing words in the blanks below. Look at the story to correct your work.

At the hospital emergency (1) _____ , a nurse

brought a wheelchair (2) _____ Rosa. Then the nurse

asked Rosa to fill (3) _____ insurance papers. Rosa

didn't (4) _____ anything about insurance, and she

didn't (5) _____ to think about it. She was

(6) _____ a lot of pain! Just then, Ana and Grandpa

(7) _____ , so Ana (8) _____ to fill out the

papers.

Conversation

H. Look at each problem below. With your classmates, decide if you *should* or *should not* go to the emergency room for each problem. Write *yes* if you think you should go and *no* if you shouldn't.

—— 1. You are coughing and sneezing.
—— 2. You fall down and can't walk.
—— 3. It is late at night. A small child in your family has a high fever and screams for four hours.
—— 4. You have a headache.
—— 5. Your brother burns his leg with very hot water.
—— 6. Your stomach hurts, but you can still walk around and go to work.

I. In the phone book, look up the following numbers. Write them in the blanks.

fire _____

rescue (ambulance) _____

police _____

doctor _____

poison center _____

Now copy the numbers on a small card and put it by your phone at home.

J. Read the problems below. With another classmate, decide which number you should call from the list above. Write the name and number in the blank.

Example: You have a bad headache.
                doctor 257-6798

1. You come home at night. Your front door is open and your TV is gone. _____

2. You think your small child drank some dishwashing soap.

   _____

3. You look out your window and see smoke coming out of your neighbor's house. _____

4. You come home and find your sister on the floor. She isn't moving or breathing. _____

5. You took some medicine for a stomachache. The medicine is all gone and you are not better. _____

Writing

K. Rosa stayed home from school for a few days after her accident. Some friends sent her a get-well card. Below are some pictures of greeting cards that Americans send to each other. On the line under each card, write the sentence that matches.

1. _____   2. _____

3. _____ 4. _____ 5. _____

1. Your friend is celebrating Christmas.
2. You want to say thank you to someone.
3. A cousin is graduating from high school.
4. Your neighbor's wife died.
5. Your friend's son is having a birthday.

Reading Practice

L. It is very important to read and understand medicine labels. Talk about the words, read the labels below, and then answer the questions about each label.

vitamins	out of reach
dosage	daily
tablet	aspirin
warning	refrigerate
teaspoon	

1.
> **ASPIRIN**
> DOSAGE: Adults take 2 tablets every 4 hours. Not for children under 12.
> WARNING: Keep out of reach of children.

Questions:

a. I take two tablets at 8:00 a.m. When can I take more? And when can I take more again?
b. Can I give these tablets to a six-year-old child?
c. Where should I put this bottle of medicine?

2.
> **VITAMINS**
> One tablet daily for adults.
> Refrigerate.
> Keep out of reach of children.

Questions:

a. How many tablets will I take each day?
b. Where should I keep this bottle?
c. Can children take these vitamins?

3.
> **CHILDREN'S PAIN MEDICINE**
> AGE: 3
> DOSAGE: 3 teaspoons, every 4 hours

Questions:

a. Who is this medicine for?
b. What is the medicine for?
c. I give my child three teaspoons at 10:00. When can I give my child more?

15

What Next?

Pre-reading

A. What does it mean? Do you know the names of the jobs in each picture above? Write the name of the job in the picture next to its number.

JOBS

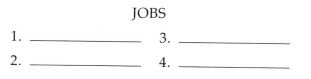

1. _____ 3. _____

2. _____ 4. _____

B. What do you think?

1. Carlos, twenty-one, is a student at a *community college*. He's thinking about his future. In five years, do you think he will be a student or have a job? How will his life change?
2. If he goes to school, how will he get money to pay for it?
3. What are *school counselors*? What do they do?

Reading

WHAT NEXT?

Carlos is talking to his counselor at the community college. Carlos is making plans for his future.

Counselor: What about next year, Carlos?

Carlos: I'm not sure what I'll do. I want to stay in school, but I also need to earn some money to help my family.

Counselor: Have you looked for a job?

Carlos: Yes, but all the jobs are for dishwashing or cleaning, and I hate washing dishes and cleaning!

Counselor: Some offices have part-time data processing jobs, and you took a data processing class last semester. Would you like that better than washing dishes?

Carlos: Much better! When can I start work?

Counselor: Wait a minute! We don't have a job for you yet. And what about finishing school?

Carlos: This is great! I'll work and go to school. Maybe I'll go to engineering school. I can't wait to tell Mom. She'll be so happy.

Counselor: Carlos, wait!

Carlos: I've changed my mind. I'll go to medical school. Dr. Carlos Gonzalez. That's nice!

Counselor: Not so fast, Doctor. First let's try to get you that data processing job.

Comprehension

C. Answer these questions about "What Next?"

1. Why is Carlos talking to a counselor?
2. Why does Carlos want a job?
3. What kind of a job does Carlos want? What kind doesn't he want?
4. What will Carlos tell Mom?
5. How do you know Carlos is excited?

D. Answer these questions. Some questions have more than one answer.

1. Carlos will work and go to school at the same time. What kind of problems might he have?
2. Do you think Carlos will go to medical school next year? Why or why not?
3. What about you? Who can help you plan for the future?

Vocabulary

E. Find a sentence on the right that means the same as a sentence on the left. Write the correct letter in the blank.

_____ 1. I can't wait to tell you.
_____ 2. I changed my mind.
_____ 3. Tell me again, but not so fast.
_____ 4. He is planning for the future.
_____ 5. Carlos will look for a job.
_____ 6. I hate cold weather.
_____ 7. What about my idea?

a. Carlos will try to find a job.
b. What do you think of my idea?
c. I don't like cold weather at all.
d. I want to tell you right away.
e. Talk more slowly.
f. I have a different idea now.
g. He is getting ready for the future.

Listening

F. Books closed. Your teacher will read these problems to you. You will hear them two times. Then answer questions about them on a piece of paper. After you answer the questions, open your book and check your answers.

1. Tom is seventeen. He doesn't work. He goes to school, but he is often absent. Tom watches a lot of TV and plays video games. His mother gives him money for movies.

   Questions

   a. How old is Tom?
   b. Does he have a job?
   c. How does he spend his time?

   Discuss this question: What would you tell Tom's mother to do about Tom?

2. Mrs. Brown works at night because she couldn't get a daytime job. She has two daughters, ages fifteen and eighteen. While their mother is working at night, they watch TV and visit with friends. Sometimes the girls are very tired, don't do their home-work, and don't go to school the next day.

   Questions

   a. When does Mrs. Brown work?
   b. How old are her daughters?
   c. What do her daughters do at night?

   Discuss this question: What can Mrs. Brown do to take care of her daughters while she is at work?

3. Lue is twenty years old. He is a good student, but he doesn't plan to go to a community college. He thinks it would be too difficult. No one in his family ever went to school.

   Questions

   a. How old is Lue?
   b. Is he a good student?
   c. Why doesn't Lue plan to go to a community college?

   Discuss this question: Is college necessary for all high school graduates? Why or why not?

Conversation

G. Talk to a classmate about your future. Ask each other the following questions about the time five years from now. Give long answers. After you work with a partner, share some of your answers with the whole class.

1. How do you feel about your future. (Scared? Excited?)
2. Will you have a job? What kind?
3. Will you still go to school? If yes, what will you study? How long will you go to school? How will you pay for school?
4. What can you do now to get ready for your life in five years? (For example: talk to a school counselor, open a savings account to save money for school.)
5. What will you do for fun?

Writing

H. Read this paragraph about the future. Carlos wrote it in English class.

IN TEN YEARS

In ten years, it will be 1997, and I will live in Milwaukee, Wisconsin. I will work as an engineer. To get ready for that job I will go to the university for five years. For fun, I will be a bicycle racer. The biggest change in my life will be getting married and having children.

Now, complete the following paragraph about your life in five years. Practice reading so you can read your paragraph to your classmates.

In five years, it will be _____, and I will live in

_____. I will work as a(n) _____. To prepare

for that job, I will _____. For fun, I will

_____. The biggest change in my life will be

_____.

I. Write the paragraph again, but start out with the words *In ten years* . . .

Reading Practice

MY MAID, THE COMPUTER

In the future, computers will help at home. There are lots of things they can do well. For example, if you want to turn on the oven, you won't need to walk all the way to the kitchen. Just tell the computer, and the computer will do it. The computer can also answer the door for you. The computer might say, "Will you wait a minute, please? Someone will be here right away."

Or if you aren't at home, just call your home. The computer will answer the phone. Then tell the computer what you want to do. The computer can start cooking for you or turn up the heat or turn on the lights.

And if there is trouble at home, the computer can call you! Is your dinner burning? Did the heat go off? Did the kids come home from school early? Is there too much noise? You'll find out right away. And when you tell the computer to do something, the computer can't say, "Sorry, I'm busy."

J. Answer these questions about "My Maid, the Computer."

1. In the future, what will you be able to tell the computer to do?
2. What will the computer tell you?
3. How are computers different from other helpers?

Irregular Verbs

Present	Past	Present	Past
be (am, are, is)	was, were	keep	kept
begin	began	know	knew
blow	blew	leave	left
break	broke	let	let
bring	brought	make	made
buy	bought	meet	met
come	came	pay	paid
do	did	put	put
drive	drove	read	read
eat	ate	run	ran
fall	fell	say	said
feel	felt	see	saw
find	found	speak	spoke
fit	fit	stand	stood
forget	forgot	take	took
get	got	tell	told
give	gave	think	thought
go	went	understand	understood
have	had	wake	woke
hold	held	write	wrote
hurt	hurt		

Word Games

The following are suggestions for reinforcing the vocabulary in the readings through simple word games. These games can be used in addition to the vocabulary exercises in the chapters and as review for quizzes or tests.

Tic-tac-toe

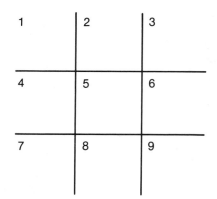

1. Draw a tic-tac-toe grid on the blackboard as illustrated. Number each square and write a vocabulary word in each one.
2. Divide the class into two teams, X and O.
3. The first player on Team X chooses a number and gives the definition of the word in the square, or uses the word in a sentence. If the player is correct, X gets the square, and play goes to Team O. If the player is incorrect, play simply goes to Team O.
4. The first team to get three X's or O's in a row is the winner.

Concentration

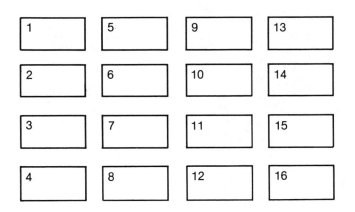

1. Write eight to ten vocabulary words on 3″ × 5″ notecards. Write synonyms for the words on separate notecards.
2. Shuffle the cards and number them on the opposite side.
3. Lay the cards out in rows with four or five cards in a row.
4. Students can be divided into teams or play individually.
5. A player turns over two cards. If they are synonyms, the player keeps them and gets another turn. If they aren't, the cards are turned back over, and play goes to the next player.
6. When all the cards have been taken, the player with the most cards is the winner.

Word Bingo

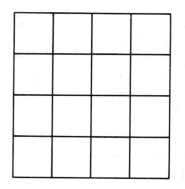

1. Make Bingo cards on 3″ × 5″ notecards by drawing sixteen to twenty squares as illustrated. Students could make the cards themselves by copying vocabulary words from the blackboard onto the squares randomly. In each square, write a vocabulary word. The order and choice of the words should be different on each card.
2. Cut out small squares of colored construction paper to use as covers for the Bingo squares.
3. Each student is given a Bingo card and some colored squares.
4. The game leader has a list of synonyms for the vocabulary words and reads them one by one to the players. If a player has the word, he or she covers it with a colored square.
5. The player who covers a row first (either horizontally or vertically) shouts "Bingo!" After the game leader verifies the "Bingo," that player is declared the winner.
6. Players can then exchange cards and play again.

Password

1. Make a list of vocabulary words on the blackboard.
2. One student (X) is chosen to leave the room.
3. The students remaining in the room choose one of the vocabulary words from the blackboard.
4. X reenters the room and sits with his or her back to the blackboard.

5. Students help X guess the word by giving synonyms.
6. When X guesses the word, another student is chosen to leave the room, and play continues.

Jeopardy

Moving In	A New Beginning	Ready to Work	Brrr
10	10	10	10
20	20	20	20
30	30	30	30
40	40	40	40
50	50	50	50

1. Draw a jeopardy board on the blackboard as illustrated. Use chapter titles for the categories and make five squares under each category. Number the squares 10, 20, 30, 40, 50. Leave the squares blank.
2. Make an identical jeopardy board on a piece of paper for the game leader. In each square, write a vocabulary word from the chapter. (The game can also be played using comprehension questions from the chapter.) The words or questions should increase in difficulty from 10 to 50 points if possible.
3. Divide the class into two teams, A and B.
4. Player 1A begins by choosing a category and a point value (for example, "Chocolate Soup, 20").
5. The game leader then says a synonym for the word (or asks the question) in that square. If player 1A gives the correct vocabulary word for that synonym, Team A gets 20 points, and play goes to Team B. If player 1A is incorrect, play simply goes to Team B.
6. When all the squares have been taken, the team with the most points wins.